SECOND GENERATION DMUS

John Jackson

AMBERLEY

First published 2019

Amberley Publishing
The Hill, Stroud
Gloucestershire, GL5 4EP

www.amberley-books.com

Copyright © John Jackson, 2019

The right of John Jackson to be identified as
the Author of this work has been asserted in
accordance with the Copyrights, Designs and
Patents Act 1988.

ISBN 978 1 4456 7596 1 (print)
ISBN 978 1 4456 7597 8 (ebook)

British Library Cataloguing in Publication Data.
A catalogue record for this book is available from
the British Library.

Origination by Amberley Publishing.
Printed in the UK.

Introduction

This book tells the latest chapter in the story of Britain's diesel multiple units (or DMUs for short). Were they unloved? Yes. Were they noisy? Also yes. Were they one of the main culprits for the end of steam on Britain's railways? Perhaps. But they also brought many advantages to our twentieth-century railways – not least because the engines were incorporated into the carriages themselves and no separate locomotive was required.

In the UK, the roots of diesel multiple units, as we know them today, can be traced back to the Great Western Railway's railcars, introduced just before the Second World War. Since then, the 1955 Modernisation Plan saw the use of diesel units expanded throughout the rail network. Their rapid introduction was chiefly a response to the need to eliminate the ongoing use of expensive steam locomotives in hauling passenger trains, particularly on branch and secondary lines.

And it was not just steam locomotives that these units replaced. Today it is taken for granted that, on almost all trains, passengers can reach all of the facilities on board. In many cases these units replaced non-corridor coaching stock, where access to such facilities was not an option. So, while enthusiasts may not have liked them, they were initially generally well received by the travelling public at large.

The result of this major power switch was a substantial fleet of several thousand rail carriages. These 'units', built in the 1950s and early 1960s, were to become known as first generation DMUs. Designs were varied and production split between a number of manufacturers, much like the building of their diesel locomotive counterparts. The units' carriages were arranged in fixed formations, ranging from a single car upwards, with two and three carriages being the norm. They also provided the flexibility to work in multiple formations, although the majority had no walkway facilities between each unit.

These units served the railways of Britain well for more than a generation. They were a major factor in many lines surviving the Beeching Axe in the mid-1960s, when the financial viability of every railway line was being put under the spotlight. Because of their much-reduced operating costs, they were a particularly important factor in this calculation as they spent much of their time running on loss-making lines. By the 1980s, however, the majority of these early types of unit were life expired and a replacement strategy was needed. By then our railways were in the hands of British Rail, and in the years running up to privatisation the UK embarked on what was to become known as 'Sprinterisation'. This was the term used to describe the widespread takeover of many services by second generation DMUs.

A few years earlier, British Rail Engineering Ltd (BREL) and Leyland had jointly developed a second generation of four-wheeled railbuses. LEV1, as it was to become known, was unveiled in 1978. Its name was derived from the initials of Leyland Experimental Vehicle and it was in effect a Leyland National bus body with two identical ends that was adapted to run on rail tracks.

From this early experimentation a range of replacement units were introduced to suit the country's varying demands for this more modern traction, with the twenty British Leyland-built Class 141 units being the first to appear in the mid-1980s. They were modified by Hunslet Barclay a few years later. Despite these modifications, life for these pioneers was to be short-lived, with them seeing less than fifteen years in service in the UK prior to withdrawal. Several units had their working lives extended following export to the railways of Iran.

The wider manufacture of second generation units was to be split between BREL and a number of other private companies, such as Metro-Cammell, who were entrusted to build the 114 two-car Class 156 units. In this book we examine the wide range of classes of diesel multiple units introduced on our railways in the period from those early 1980s years through to the present day, almost forty years later.

Unloved as these units may have been half a century ago, that is nothing compared to attitudes today. Most users of the first classes of these later generation of diesel units agree that the ride quality leaves a lot to be desired, particularly over points and when rounding tight curves – the trackwork does not suit the bus-style bench seating. This is particularly true of the Class 142 'Pacers', a variant built by BREL, which have acquired the nickname of 'Nodding Donkeys'. On a more universal front, our passion for protecting our planet's environment from the fumes these units emit has moved our rail industry away from these diesel-powered units and firmly in the direction of electric-powered ones.

These units are required to run on electrified lines, of course. Today, where that can't be done quickly or economically, 'bi-mode' has become a buzzword when thinking of solutions. This means the operators can run the same unit in electric-power mode wherever possible, using its diesel motors only as a fallback. Back in 1990, BREL built a substantial fleet of Class 319 electric multiple units. Thirty-five of these four-car trains are in the process of conversion to bi-mode by Brush Traction at Loughborough. And, as I write this introduction, the word 'tri-mode' has even entered railway vocabulary. First Great Western are exploring the possible use of flexible units that can operate under diesel power, 750 V DC third rail and 25 kV AC overhead electric power.

Some of those die-hard enthusiasts saddened at the passing of their precious steam trains take a nostalgic view of the first generation units now consigned to history and to preserved lines across the country. Only time will tell as to whether or not their second (and third) generation counterparts will form part of tomorrow's nostalgia market.

In the meantime, let's take a more in-depth look at the second generation diesel multiple units in use on our railways as the second decade of the twenty-first century draws to a close.

Gone are the days when all units carried the familiar BR green and then blue liveries. Today, our unit fleet is distributed in revenue-earning service across most of our UK train operators, resulting in a multitude of liveries on display. In this book I have attempted to include as many examples of these liveries as possible, across the many types of units that carry them. That said, with franchises changing hands regularly, keeping abreast of resultant livery changes is quite a challenge – particularly where operators have recognised the opportunity to use their rolling stock for advertising and promotional purposes.

Gone, too, are slam-door units and the ability for the customer to open the unit's windows. Today's railways are more conscious of air conditioning, health and safety issues and station 'dwell times'. As a regular user of 'Meridians' on the Midland Main Line, I can vouch for the drawbacks these units have when it comes to passenger loading and unloading, particularly at busy times.

For the sake of convenience, I have not attempted to place the units featured in this book in the order of their chronological introduction to service. Rather, breaking with my tradition in previous books, the units contained in the pages that follow have been placed in numeric order from the Class 139 Parry People Movers through to the Class 222 units. There's a glimpse of the Class 230 unit at the rear of the book, too.

From the 1990s, there had been a steady delivery of new classes of diesel multiple units for the numerous operators of the post-privatisation railway. This came to a halt in 2010/11 following the completion of the Class 172 Turbostar units, built by Bombardier.

After a gap of almost a decade, one of today's operators, Northern by Arriva, is about to take delivery of the first of their fleet of Class 195 diesel multiple units for the much-heralded Northern Connect services. Twenty-five two-car and thirty three-car units are being assembled in Irún in Spain. Sadly, no photographs of these are yet available.

Nevertheless, I hope that you enjoy your journey through these pages as much as I have enjoyed compiling them.

John Jackson

Class 121

It seems appropriate to mark the end of the era of first generation diesel multiple units at the start of this book. The end for two long-term survivors came in May 2017. From this date, Chiltern Railways withdrew its two Class 121 'bubble cars', dating back to 1960, from its Princes Risborough to Aylesbury service. This withdrawal also heralded the end of vacuum-braked trains on the network. Unit No. 121020 is seen on 15 April 2017, shortly before withdrawal, while stabled at its home depot of Aylesbury. This unit now has a new life in preservation on the Bodmin & Wenford Railway.

LEV1

In 1978, the LEV1 was introduced. This Leyland Experimental Vehicle was evaluated in passenger service, although it carried a departmental coaching stock number, RDB975874. This early photograph, dating from around 1980, was taken while the unit was stabled between duties in Platform 4 at Ipswich station.

Class 139

In 2009, London Midland commenced operation of its fleet of two Class 139 Parry People Movers (PPMs). These single carriage units, which run on a small onboard LPG-fuelled engine, have a maximum speed of 20 mph. On 3 July 2013, No. 139002 waits for passengers to board at Stourbridge Town station.

The PPM units alternate in service on the branch from here to Stourbridge Junction station, approximately ¾ mile away. The ten-minute interval service connects there with other local services in the West Midlands, notably towards Birmingham. On 11 October 2014, sister unit No. 139001 waits at Stourbridge Junction to return to Town station. The units' home depot is the small shed in the background.

Class 141

This class of two-car units was to be the first of the 'Pacer' models. Twenty of these units were manufactured by Leyland in the mid-1980s. They were modified by Hunslet Barclay some five years later in order to improve reliability. On 19 September 1993, No. 141109 stands at Sheffield, in between duties.

These units were allocated to Neville Hill depot (Leeds) and were used on services that operated out of the nearby City station. The fleet was withdrawn at the end of the twentieth century, with eight examples being exported for use on the railways of Iran. Unit No. 141113 was a UK survivor, entering into preservation. It is owned by the Llangollen Railcar Group, although it was to be seen at the Midland Railway Centre in Butterley on 14 September 2013.

Class 142

A total of ninety-six Class 142 units were built by British Rail Engineering Ltd at Derby in the mid-1980s. Fifteen of these units are operated by Arriva Trains Wales (ATW), predominantly on their services on the Valley Lines. On 9 November 2017, No. 142006 is partnered with No. 142077 as they wait at Merthyr Tydfil on a service to Barry Island.

The bus-style seating and layout of these Pacer units can clearly be seen in this view of car No. 55547, from set No. 142006.

These ATW units make occasional forays into England. On 13 November 2017, No. 142010 makes a call at Severn Tunnel Junction on an England-bound service to Cheltenham Spa.

Two units from this class have been withdrawn following accident damage. No. 142059, suffering from braking problems, collided with the buffer stops at Liverpool Lime Street in 1991 and, eight years later, No. 142008 was involved in a collision with a Virgin express at Winsford. This leaves a balance of seventy-nine units in service with Northern by Arriva. On 17 June 2013, No. 142025 calls at Newcastle Central on one of Northern's services in the North East. It is forming a service along the Tyne Valley to Hexham.

Newton Heath in Manchester is the home depot for many of the Northern units. On 26 October 2014, Nos 142034 (on the left) and 142013 (on the right) are seen stabled there between passenger duties.

These Manchester-based units provide services covering a wide area of northern England. On 21 March 2018, No. 142048 calls at Edale in Derbyshire's Peak District while operating a Hope Valley stopping service from Manchester to Sheffield.

Northern are supporters of the 'Movember' campaign to raise awareness of men's health issues. On 12 November 2014, No. 142062 stands at Chester, complete with a front-end moustache for 'Movember'.

A fleet of these Northern units are allocated to their depot at Heaton, near Newcastle. They can also be found on services throughout the north-east of England. On 16 April 2018, No. 142065 calls at Marske, near Middlesbrough, on a Bishop Auckland to Saltburn service.

The new operator of services in Wales has promised a transformation of rail travel across the country, including in the South Wales Valleys. With its days possibly numbered, No. 142083 calls at Ynyswen on a service to Treherbert on 9 November 2017.

Leeds is another base for the Class 142 Northern by Arriva units, with units being stabled at nearby Neville Hill depot. On 25 November 2015, No. 142084 waits to leave City station on a stopping service to Huddersfield.

On the western side of the Pennines, No. 142093 is paired with a Class 150 unit, No. 150275, as it calls at Leyland on a service to St Helens Central. All of these units are scheduled for withdrawal by the end of 2019 as they do not comply with the UK's 2010 Rail Vehicle Accessibility Regulations.

Class 143

Twenty-five units of this class of Pacers were built by Hunslet Barclay at Kilmarnock and numbered 143001–25 when new. These two-car units originally saw service in North East England, subsequently being transferred in the early 1990s to South Wales and South West England. On 8 November 2017, No. 143602 waits at Ebbw Vale Town, forming a service to Cardiff Central.

These units share duties on the South Wales Valley Lines with both Class 142s and Class 150s. On 8 November 2017, No. 143609 waits to leave Bargoed and take the single-line section to Rhymney. Unusually for Arriva Trains Wales, this unit is named, carrying the name of one of Wales's favourite countrymen, *Sir Tom Jones*.

Two of these Class 143 units have been victims of fire damage and subsequent withdrawal, namely No. 143613 in 2004 and No. 143615 a year later. The remaining units are currently allocated to Arriva Trains Wales (fifteen units) and Great Western Railway (eight units). On 26 May 2014, the latter operator's No. 143617 is stabled in the bay at Exeter St Davids, awaiting its next duty.

The Great Western Railway units are serviced at the depots at Exeter and St Philip's Marsh, Bristol. On 24 May 2015, No. 143621 is seen on the depot at Exeter with unit No. 150124 as company.

The Arriva Trains Wales fleet are used alongside Class 142 and Class 150 units, on services around Cardiff and the Valley Lines in particular. On 16 July 2015, No. 143623 leaves Cardiff's Queen Street station on the rear of a working to Penarth.

Class 144

This variant of the Pacer family was built by British Rail Engineering Ltd in 1986/87, specifically for the West Yorkshire Passenger Transport Executive. These units are now employed on Northern by Arriva services, and are allocated to their Neville Hill depot in Leeds. On 8 February 2017, No. 144007 arrives at Doncaster on a Lincoln to Scunthorpe (via Sheffield) service.

Thirteen of these Class 144 units are formed of two-car sets, including No. 144009, which is seen here approaching Barnetby on a working from Sheffield to Cleethorpes on 7 July 2018. Northern operate a Saturday-only service using the Brigg line.

A further ten units, numbered 144014–23, are formed of three cars. On 13 June 2013, one of these, No. 144019, leaves Leeds on a service to Huddersfield.

These units are employed on services throughout Yorkshire, and occasionally beyond. On 22 March 2017, No. 144022 stands at Wakefield's Kirkgate station on a service to Sheffield.

Class 150/0

In the mid-1980s, British Rail Engineering Ltd produced two prototype Class 150 'Sprinter' units based on the Mark 3 coaching stock bodyshell design, Nos 150001 and 150002. Thirty years later these two units remain in service and are operated by First Great Western Railway. On 14 July 2014, No. 150001 waits at Basingstoke to form a service to Reading.

These two units have spent most of their working lives in the Midlands, and more recently on the Reading to Basingstoke service. They are now based at St Philip's Marsh, Bristol. On 29 May 2017, No. 150002 (now in Great Western Railway green livery) stands at the western outpost of Penzance, waiting to form the 11.41 service to Plymouth.

Class 150/1

An order for a further fifty two-car units was placed with BREL and these were to become Class 150/1. They were numbered from No. 150101 to No. 150150 with delivery from 1985 onwards. The first of the subclass, No. 150101, is seen here in Central Trains' livery on 21 May 1996 as it calls at Duffield on a Derby to Matlock service.

In more recent years, examples of the class have been working on First Great Western's services, particularly in the West Country. On the evening of 30 May 2017, No. 150104 calls at Par station on the 20.19 service to Plymouth. Meanwhile, sister unit No. 150130 *Severnside Community Rail Partnership* waits in the bay platform to form the last train of the day (20.28) to Newquay.

A small fleet of the class are retained by London Midland (now London North Western) for services including the Marston Vale line between Bletchley and Bedford. On 12 November 2016, No. 150107 is seen near Stewartby.

The majority of the Class 150/1 units are currently in service with Northern by Arriva, operating across most of the north of England. On 17 May 2018, No. 150112 arrives at Leeds on a service from York (via the Harrogate loop).

These units can still be seen operating some diagrams to and from Merseyside. On 18 September 2013, No. 150145 is seen leaving Southport on a service to Manchester Airport.

Northern's Class 150 units share in the operation of services from Manchester to Buxton. On 21 March 2015, it's the turn of No. 150150 to leave Manchester Piccadilly and head for the Derbyshire terminus.

Class 150/2

The final Sprinter Class 150 variant was to be the Class 150/2. A total of eighty-five units were built, with front end gangway connections enabling passengers to move between units when they were working in multiple. Back in 1997, unit No. 150207 sported Regional Railways livery as it called at Manchester Piccadilly on 18 October that year.

Arriva Trains Wales (ATW) currently operates a fleet of thirty-four of these two-car units on services in both the Welsh Valleys and further afield. On 9 November 2017, No. 150213 calls at Ninian Park station on a City Line service.

Further afield, No. 150235 is found on an ATW service operating wholly within England, having just arrived at Crewe on a service from Chester on 18 June 2014. One of these Class 150 units is employed throughout the day, shuttling between these two railway interchanges.

In North Wales, Class 150/2s are regular performers on the Conwy Valley services between Llandudno and Blaenau Ffestiniog. On 14 June 2018, No. 150240 skirts the Conwy Estuary as it calls at the request stop at Glan Conwy.

First Great Western Railway also uses Class 150/2 on a variety of services in the west of its operating area. On 28 May 2016, No. 150247 is seen leaving Exeter St Davids on a service to Barnstaple. It has a Class 153 for company.

The same unit, No. 150247, is also seen in Devon, almost a quarter of a century earlier. On 22 September 1994, then sporting Regional Railways livery, the unit is seen skirting the coast as it heads west through Dawlish.

A number of Northern units sport a 'Welcome to Yorkshire' promotional livery. One such example, No. 150271, is seen on the rear of a service bound for Southport as it arrives at Manchester Piccadilly on 4 June 2015.

That Yorkshire promotional branding on sister unit No. 150275 has since been replaced. It is now in traffic carrying Northern by Arriva's latest livery. On 1 October 2017, it arrives at Leyland, near Preston, with a Class 142 unit as its partner.

Northern Class 150 units make occasional visits to Nottingham on services to and from Leeds. On 19 July 2016, No. 150276 calls at Chesterfield on a southbound service. This unit also carried the 'Welcome to Yorkshire' vinyls at the time.

For several years now, train operators have suffered a shortage of diesel units to work local services in East Anglia. On 8 June 2012, ATW-operated unit No. 150280 was on hire to cover one such Anglian diagram. It is seen far away from home, calling at Hoveton & Wroxham on a local service between Sheringham and Norwich.

On the opposite side of the country, sister unit No. 150285 is on more familiar ATW territory. It is seen on 11 November 2017, waiting to leave the West Wales terminus at Pembroke Dock on a service to Swansea.

Class 150/9

These Class 150 units often get split as a result of exams or damage to individual cars. These 'hybrid units' are usually so formed by First Great Western and renumbered as Class 150/9s. One such example, No. 150925, operated as a three-car (two-car unit No. 150125 with middle car No. 57209 added) when seen here approaching Severn Tunnel Junction. The date is 13 November 2017 and the unit is working a Taunton to Cardiff service.

A total of seventy single-carriage Class 153 units operate across most of the UK with a number of different operators. They were originally built by Leyland as two-car (Class 155) units, and were later separated. On 6 July 2016, Northern's No. 153301 awaits its next duty at the buffer stops at Leeds City.

These Northern units are often used to strengthen services, typically working with two coach units to make a three-car rake. Here, unit No. 153307 has just arrived at Leeds City station on the rear of a service from Manchester Victoria on 17 May 2017.

A small pool of five units are operated by Greater Anglia from their Norwich Crown Point depot. These are found on branch services based on both Norwich and Ipswich. On 29 September 2016, two of these units, Nos 153309 *Gerard Fiennes* and No. 153314, are captured at the buffer stops in Norwich station.

In a former 'One' livery, No. 153314 is seen in East Anglia almost a decade earlier, on 28 August 2007, while calling at Ely.

Arriva Trains Wales uses a small fleet of these units across most of its territory. This includes operating most of the shuttle services on the Cardiff Bay branch to and from Cardiff Queen Street. On 16 July 2015, No. 153320 has just arrived at Queen Street.

A single Class 153 unit can often be seen on the stopping service operating between Crewe and Shrewsbury. In an earlier Arriva Trains Wales livery, No. 153323 is seen at Crewe on 30 October 2014, waiting to return to Shrewsbury.

Dating back to the days of Regional Railways, No. 153334 calls at Retford's Low Level platforms on 4 August 1992 while forming a service to Sheffield. This unit is now operated by West Midlands Trains.

East Midlands Trains (EMT) has a pool of these Class 153 units, increasing in size with transfers from the West Country. They operate across most of EMT's franchise, including several routes in the Lincolnshire area. On 13 February 2018, No. 153355 calls at Gainsborough's Lea Road station on a Doncaster to Lincoln working.

London Midland maintain a fleet of eight Class 153 units. Their duties include strengthening services on the Birmingham to Walsall and Rugeley services. On 5 May 2017, No. 153365, accompanied by No. 170504, is seen approaching Bescot Stadium on a Walsall-bound service.

These London Midland units are also used alongside their Class 150 stablemates on Marston Vale branch services between Bletchley and Bedford. On 23 June 2016, No. 153371 is seen leaving Bletchley.

Units from the West Country are also being transferred to Northern. On 23 August 2018, newly arrived No. 153373 is paired with No. 153360 as it approaches Doncaster station. Unit No. 153373 currently retains its Great Western Railway green livery, with all former branding having been removed.

Class 155

The Class 153 units were originally delivered as Class 155 two-car units. Regional Railways-liveried No. 155333, which became individual Class 153 unit numbers No. 153333 and No. 153383 on separation, arrives at Cardiff Central on 12 October 1991.

A small fleet of seven units were retained as Class 155s in two-car formation. They were originally built for the West Yorkshire Passenger Transport Executive as Metro trains, and are currently operated by Northern. On 17 May 1995, and in original Metro colours, No. 155341 is seen reversing at Bradford Interchange on a Leeds to Halifax service.

On 11 April 2018, sister unit No. 155346 is among the first to be outshopped in new Northern by Arriva livery, having arrived on a service from Manchester Victoria. It waits at Leeds station between duties.

Class 156

Pioneer unit No. 156401 was newly delivered at the end of 1987. After numerous changes of both operator and livery, it is on the books of East Midlands Trains (EMT) and is seen arriving at Lincoln on a terminating service from Leicester thirty years later, on 21 September 2017.

Back on 24 May 1991, No. 156404, then in Provincial livery, calls at Loughborough on a working to Great Yarmouth.

More than two decades later, on 15 May 2013, the same unit calls at the same station. It is now in EMT livery and working a local 'Ivanhoe' stopping service from Leicester to Lincoln.

The first thirty Class 156 units to be delivered were all allocated to Norwich before being transferred away. Nine of these units were to return to the Anglia Region early this century when they were swapped with a similar number of Class 150 units. On 7 September 2017, one such returnee, No. 156416, is seen operating a Greater Anglia (GA) branch service at Reedham.

These GA units also work branch services out of Ipswich. On 7 September 2017, No. 156417 approaches Beccles while working the 15.25 service to Lowestoft.

Northern by Arriva operate a substantial fleet of Class 156s across the whole of their North of England franchise area. These duties include their use on the majority of services on the Cumbrian Coast line between Carnforth, Barrow, Whitehaven and Carlisle. On 15 June 2018, No. 156426 is seen passing Drigg signal box on a Barrow to Carlisle service.

These Cumbrian Coast services terminate at Carlisle and, on 9 April 2015, No. 156429 arrives here on a service from Barrow-in-Furness. These units are scheduled to make this 85-mile journey in around two and a half hours.

These Northern Class 156 units regularly work as far south as Derbyshire's Peak District. On 20 March 2018, No. 156440 *George Bradshaw* is the rear unit as it stands at Buxton on a morning commuter services to Manchester and beyond to Preston.

On 18 April 2018, No. 156443 is seen at Newton Aycliffe while working a Darlington to Bishop Auckland service. This unit also carries the new Northern by Arriva livery.

Nearly fifty of the 114 Class 156 units are currently in service with ScotRail and are based at their depot at Corkerhill in Glasgow. On 7 October 2017, a pair of units, Nos 156449 (nearest camera) and No. 156457, are seen at Stirling on an Alloa to Glasgow Queen Street service.

Fifteen of the Scottish units are Radio Electronic Token Block (RETB)-fitted to enable them to work over the West Highland Line. This covers the area linking Glasgow to Fort William and Mallaig, together with the section from Crianlarich to Oban. No. 156450 is one of the units so fitted, and is seen here at Crianlarich on 15 April 2017. There's just a hint of snow left on the moor tops.

Further north, a pair of RETB-fitted units, No. 156453 paired with No. 156447, are seen on a service from Mallaig to Fort William on 6 May 2015. The location is the famous Glenfinnan Viaduct.

Twenty-five years earlier, these units also worked the lines north of Inverness. On 28 June 1993, No. 156477, which is still a Corkerhill-based unit, is seen arriving at Muir of Ord station.

In May 2011, four Class 156 units were transferred from Northern to East Midlands Trains. Two of these, Nos 156498 and 156497, are seen departing from Wainfleet on a Nottingham to Skegness service on 7 July 2018.

The ScotRail Class 156s also work services in southern Scotland and are the regular performers on the non-electrified lines from Glasgow to Carlisle via Dumfries. On 18 October 2017, No. 156507 passes Floriston level crossing, just north of Kingmoor Yard, Carlisle, on a service bound for Glasgow Central.

Class 158

All Class 158 units were built by BREL at Derby, with the first units being deployed by British Rail in Scotland from 1990 onwards. On 25 June 1999, No. 158702, then named *BBC Scotland*, is seen waiting at Inverness.

On 24 May 1990, recently built No. 158703 is seen in Derby station on a test run. The destination panel optimistically states 'Glasgow via Shotts'.

Class 158 units were once the mainstay of services on the Highland Line. In recent years they have been chiefly displaced by the Class 170s. They are now confined to diagrams enabling unit swaps between Inverness and Edinburgh Haymarket depots. On 23 July 2013, No. 158732 is seen heading a southbound service near Dalnacardoch, north of Blair Atholl.

Northern by Arriva operate a fleet of Class 158s. These are chiefly two-car units, but they also have eight three-car formations on their books. These include No. 158754, which, on 26 October 2015, had just terminated at Manchester's Victoria station.

East Midlands Trains also operate a fleet of Class 158s, which are based at their depot at Nottingham Eastcroft. They are the regular performers on the route from Liverpool to Norwich, covering the distance of just over 250 miles in around five and a half hours. Single units operate the Nottingham to Norwich leg, as evidenced here with No. 158773 heading east through Shippea Hill on 2 May 2015. Later that year, the unit was to be named *Eastcroft Depot*.

Nineteen units are operated by Arriva Trains Wales from their depot at Machynlleth. They are employed on Central Wales services between Pwllheli, Aberystwyth and the West Midlands. On 7 July 2014, No. 158826 leads a pair of units on a service from Birmingham International as it approaches Smethwick Galton Bridge.

Northern unit No. 158849 was chosen to receive promotional vinyls in 2014. Its branding recognised that the first two stages of the Tour de France were being run in Yorkshire. The unit is seen in Sheffield on 10 September that year.

A small fleet of two-car Class 158 units is operated by South Western Railway from its Salisbury depot. On 24 May 2014, one of these units, No. 158880, is seen stabled in its home depot.

Class 158/9

A final batch of ten two-car Class 158 units were built specifically for the West Yorkshire Passenger Transport Executive for use on Metro services around Leeds. These have since been incorporated into Northern's fleet, although they remain unnumbered. On 25 October 2015, No. 158905 is seen arriving at Skipton while working a Carlisle to Leeds service.

A fleet of eighteen two-car units were reformed into three-car sets for use by Great Western Railway (as it is now) and were renumbered in the 158/9 series. The cab in the centre car is locked out of use. They work primarily on the Cardiff to Portsmouth Harbour route. On 10 November 2017, No. 158956 enters Cardiff Central station in readiness to form a service to Portsmouth.

Class 159/0

A fleet of twenty-two Class 158 units, ordered by Regional Railways and built by BREL at Derby in the late 1980s, were modified for use by Network SouthEast. They were to become Class 159s and replace loco-hauled stock on the Waterloo to Salisbury, Yeovil and Exeter route. On 25 June 2014, No. 159003 *Templecombe* heads through Clapham Junction on a West of England-bound service.

These West of England services are now in the hands of South Western Railway, and their livery is being applied to these units at Brush works in Loughborough. On 18 March 2018, No. 159007 is returning to its home depot at Salisbury when seen passing through Nuneaton station.

The entire fleet of Class 159 units are maintained at South Western Railway's depot at Salisbury. On 24 May 2014, in the South West Trains' franchise era, No. 159017 stands at the buffer stops in the sidings next to its home depot.

On 4 April 1996, back in the days of British Rail's Network SouthEast operations, No. 159019 is seen at the buffer stops at London Waterloo. It had just arrived on a service from Salisbury.

Almost twenty years later, on 25 June 2014, sister No. 159020, as a South West Trains unit, is also seen on a Salisbury to Waterloo service as it passes through Clapham Junction station.

Class 159/1

In 2007, a further eight of these three-car Class 159 units were formed using redundant TransPennine Express cars. These were to be numbered Nos 159101–8. On 2 June 2013, No. 159106 stands at Exeter St Davids, waiting to form a service to London Waterloo.

On 2 June 2017, No. 159107 (along with No. 159015) stands in the bay platform at Salisbury. Units on London to Exeter services are often joined or split here.

These units also stable at Clapham Junction between duties. On 3 December 2015, No. 159108 leads a rake of nine coaches stabled there for servicing between duties. They will work ECS into Waterloo to work evening peak services.

Class 165/0

The Class 165 'Turbo' units were built by BREL at its York works in the early 1990s and were originally delivered to British Rail's Network SouthEast's Thames and Chiltern services. Today, twenty-eight two-car and eleven three-car units are currently operated by Chiltern Railways. On 24 May 2013, two-car unit No. 165001 calls at West Ruislip.

These units have started to appear in 'Chiltern by Arriva' livery. On 9 May 2018, a spotless No. 165005 is seen sporting its new look at Leamington Spa.

One of Chiltern Railways' eleven three-car units, No. 165031 is seen waiting in London's Marylebone station on 10 September 2015.

On 29 June 2015, a five-car rake of empty coaching stock passes through Wembley Stadium station. Three-car unit No. 165035 is on the rear of this pairing (nearest the camera).

Class 165/1

As with their Chiltern Class 165/0 counterparts, these units were also a split of two- and three-car units. Thirty-seven units were built, originally for Network SouthEast, with seventeen being two-car and twenty being three-car units. Today they are operated by Great Western Railways (GWR). On 16 June 2015, No. 165109 passes through Acton Main Line on a Paddington-bound service.

GWR's green livery is being applied to these units. On 14 November 2017, another three-car unit, No. 165113, is seen sporting its new colours at South Moreton, east of Didcot Parkway.

On 23 February 2018, a two-car unit in First Great Western colours, No. 165126, is seen passing Hinksey Yard, south of Oxford, on a local southbound service.

On 11 May 2017, the impressive roof of London's Paddington station is the backdrop for unit No. 165130 as it waits at the buffer stops for its next duty.

Class 166

Delivery of a fleet of twenty-one Class 166 units followed soon after their Class 165 counterparts. These air-conditioned variants were, like the Class 165/1s, capable of a maximum speed of 90 mph, and were suitable as replacements for both ageing first generation DMUs and loco-hauled passenger trains along the Great Western Main Line. In this 1992 view, and wearing Network SouthEast livery, No. 166205 also stands under the roof of Paddington station.

Almost a quarter of a century later, and in GWR green livery, three-car No. 166210 is seen approaching Reading station on 13 July 2016.

Electrification at the eastern (London) end of their network has seen many of these units displaced and moved under the control of Bristol's St Philip's Marsh depot. On 22 February 2018, No. 166214 is seen arriving at Bristol Temple Meads on a Severn Beach service.

The newly applied livery of GWR green is in evidence at Reading on 13 July 2016 with both Nos 166218 and 166214, waiting to work services to London Paddington.

Class 168/0

The Class 168s, known as Clubman units, first entered service in 1998, with the first five units being classified as Class 168/0. They were originally delivered as three-car units and were later strengthened to four cars. Although the units' implementation was planned by BR's Network SouthEast, they were delivered to Chiltern Railways in the early days of post-privatisation on the UK's railways. On 2 October 2013, No. 168004 passes through Tyseley on a Birmingham to London Marylebone service.

Class 168/1

Next to arrive, in 2000, were eight units that were designated as Class 168/1. This Chiltern Railways order was for two four-car units and six three-car units. On 20 February 2018, three-car unit No. 168111 heads through King's Sutton on a northbound service.

Class 168/2

Four years later, six units were delivered as Class 168/2. This delivery for Chiltern Railways consisted of three three-car and three four-car units. One of the four-car units in this batch, No. 168217, calls at Leamington Spa on 9 May 2017 while working a service to London Marylebone.

Class 168/3

These units started life as Class 170/3s in service with various operators including South West Trains and First TransPennine Express. They were transferred to Chiltern Railways in 2015/16 and were redesignated as Class 168/3s, being numbered Nos 168321–9. On 17 August 2018, No. 168327 passes King's Sutton on a northbound service.

Class 170/1

The Class 170 units were built by Adtranz, now Bombardier Transportation. Back in 1998, Midland Mainline took delivery of seventeen of these Class 170/1 units for its stopping services between London St Pancras, Leicester, Derby and Nottingham. In 2000, No. 170106, one of ten three-car units, calls at Market Harborough on a service to St Pancras. It carried the popular 'teal and tangerine' branding at the time.

These units were subsequently used by Central Trains before becoming part of the CrossCountry Trains fleet in a franchise shake-up in 2007. On 18 August 2018, No. 170108 is seen approaching Manea on a service from Stansted Airport to Birmingham New Street.

CrossCountry's fleet of Class 170/1 units also includes seven two-car sets. One of these, No. 170111, approaches Cardiff Central station on 10 November 2017. It is about to form a service to Nottingham, via Birmingham New Street.

Class 170/2

Eastern England has seen twelve units of this subclass being operated by various franchise holders since their delivery. Eight three-car units were delivered in 1999. One of these, No. 170206, is seen on 20 July 2017 arriving at Stowmarket while working an Ipswich to Cambridge service.

A revised Greater Anglia livery is now appearing on these units. On 23 May 2017, No. 170208 arrives at Norwich on a service from Cambridge.

A further four units were delivered in 2002. These two-car units were intended for services on the Cambridge to Norwich route, but are, in practice, used across the East of England branch lines. On 12 December 2017, No. 170271 approaches Three Horseshoes, near Turves (Cambridgeshire), on a service from Ipswich to Peterborough.

Class 170/3

As previously mentioned, some units of this subclass were subsequently redesignated as Class 168/3s. While in action with First Trans Pennine Express, No. 170306 calls at Sheffield on 26 April 2016. These Cleethorpes to Manchester Airport services were formed of two-car units, usually operating in pairs.

Four units of this subclass, Nos 170393–6, were transferred from sister company Hull Trains for service with ScotRail. One of these three-car units, No. 170393, is seen calling at Bridge of Allan on 7 October 2017. It is working the 1216 service to Glasgow Queen Street.

CrossCountry also received a pair of Class 170/3 units, Nos 170397 and 170398, on the ending of the Central Trains franchise. One of these units, No. 170397, calls at Leicester on 17 January 2017 while working a Birmingham New Street to Stansted Airport service.

Unit No. 170399 was a one-off two-car unit that was used by Porterbrook Leasing for spot hire by train operators. And it had a number! It has also been renumbered firstly to No. 170309 and then to No. 168329. Bearing its original number, and an unfamiliar Central Trains livery, it is seen calling at Tamworth Low Level on 11 March 2003.

Class 170/4

For many years ScotRail has been the operator with the largest fleet of Class 170s. In addition to the four Class 170/3s referred to above, their three-car units are mainly classified and numbered in the Class 170/4 range. On 9 October 2017, No. 170403 is seen on a southbound service from Inverness on the Highland Line. The photograph was taken at Drumochter, which, at 1,484 feet, is the highest point on the UK rail network.

In recent years these units have operated most services between Scotland's main cities. On 5 April 2015, No. 170414 is seen arriving at Perth on a service from Glasgow Queen Street to Aberdeen. This unit was chosen to receive vinyls promoting the recently reopened Scottish Borders Railway to Tweedbank.

ScotRail's units, including the Class 170s, are receiving a revised livery that has earned the nickname 'Spotrail'. It is dark blue with grey doors and incorporates a white dotted 'Saltire' (the Scottish flag) at the cab door ends. On 5 October 2017, No. 170425 arrives at Haymarket while carrying this livery.

These units have all but been replaced from their core Edinburgh Waverley to Glasgow Queen Street services. Electrification has seen them being superseded by electric multiple units. On 14 October 2013, they were the mainstay of the route. On that day, No. 170433 arrives at Haymarket on a Glasgow to Edinburgh Service. At that time it carried the First logo and branding on its cab buffers.

These units also work alongside ScotRail's Class 158s on services on the Fife Circle to and from Edinburgh Waverley. On 5 October 2017, No. 170461 is Edinburgh-bound as it calls at Burntisland.

Nine units were ordered by Strathclyde Partnership for Transport, although their operation has since been incorporated into ScotRail. They were SPT-branded when new and No. 170477 is seen on 6 January 2012 at Glasgow Queen Street in these colours. They have since received the regular ScotRail livery. With the forthcoming replacement of these units by former First Great Western HSTs on some services, sixteen Class 170s units are in the process of being transferred to Northern by Arriva.

Class 170/5

Twenty-three two-car units were operated by Central Trains. When this franchise was broken up, seventeen of these units passed to London Midland, now West Midland Trains. On 8 December 2015, a pair of these units, with No. 170514 leading, approaches Smethwick Galton Bridge on a Shrewsbury to Birmingham New Street service.

The 'Chase' line between Walsall and Rugeley Trent Valley is currently being electrified. This will see the Class 170 units displaced by electric multiple units on the West Midlands Trains' services linking the stations along the route with Birmingham. On 18 July 2016, No. 170516 leaves Rugeley's Trent Valley station as it heads towards Birmingham New Street. The closed power station is in the background.

The remaining six units passed to CrossCountry Trains. One of them, No. 170520, is seen calling at Tamworth High Level on 3 September 2002 while in operation with its former operator, Central Trains.

Today, these units carry CrossCountry livery. On 18 August 2018, No. 170521 leads No. 170115 east through Manea. The pair are working a service from Birmingham New Street to Stansted Airport.

Class 170/6

A further ten three-car units were in use with Central Trains until the end of that franchise. This pool of units was then split and the ten units were reallocated between London Midland (LM) and CrossCountry. One of the six in use with LM, No. 170631, is seen at Great Malvern on 15 February 2016.

These units are employed on a number of services on non-electrified lines around Birmingham. Another of the LM-operated units, No. 170632, is seen approaching Codsall on 1 July 2017 while working a Birmingham New Street to Shrewsbury service.

The remaining four units form part of CrossCountry Trains' pool of Class 170s. On 21 February 2018, No. 170636 is seen passing Severn Tunnel Junction on a Nottingham to Cardiff Central service.

Class 171/4

These units, which are variants of the Class 170s above, are in operation with Southern (Govia Thameslink Railway). They are fitted with Dellner couplers, enabling rescue by Class 377 electric units in an emergency. After a recent conversion following transfer from ScotRail in 2016, No. 171402 is seen at London Bridge on 3 April 2017.

Class 171/7

This subclass now totals ten two-car units. These units' area of operation includes the Marshlink service from Ashford to Hastings. More recently, that service has been extended to Brighton. On 9 October 2013, No. 171726 arrives at the Sussex resort on a service from Ashford.

These two-car units are also used to strengthen services on the non-electrified line from Uckfield into London Bridge. On 1 July 2013, No. 171728 approaches London Bridge on an afternoon off-peak service. It will be used to strengthen a return peak-hour working.

Class 171/8

Six Class 171 variants were delivered as four-car units, specifically for these Uckfield services, with train lengths strengthened during the peak periods. On 9 November 2016, No. 171801 stands in London Bridge, waiting to form an Uckfield service. One, or possibly two, two-car Class 171/1 units will be put on the front to form a six-car rake on this peak-hour service.

Class 172/0

In 2010, Bombardier in Derby provided London Overground with a fleet of eight two-car units. These were to replace Class 150 units on the services between Gospel Oak and Barking (the 'GOBLIN'). On 12 June 2015, No. 172001 calls at Leytonstone High Road on a typical GOBLIN service.

Electrification has now taken place on the GOBLIN line and the Class 172/0 units will soon be displaced by Class 710 electric units. The units are provisionally destined to transfer to the West Midlands. The DMU fleet have hitherto been maintained at Willesden depot. On 1 November 2016, a single car from unit No. 172007 can be seen outside this maintenance depot.

Class 172/1

In the same Bombardier Transportation order, four more units were delivered to Chiltern Railways. These were classified as Class 172/1 units, with two cars. On 10 September 2015, one of them, No. 172104, calls at Wembley Stadium on a Marylebone to High Wycombe service.

Class 172/2

Twelve two-car units were also delivered to London Midland, now West Midlands Trains, chiefly on services based on Birmingham's Snow Hill station. On 2 October 2013, No. 172214 is seen awaiting departure from Snow Hill station.

Unlike the 172/0 and 172/1 variants, these units are gangwayed, aiding multiple working with passenger and staff movements between sets. A pair of two-car units, with No. 172218 leading, calls at Smethwick Galton Bridge on 20 September 2013.

The same unit is seen again on 14 March 2013. This time it is on the rear of a four-car working as the pair of two-car units leave Birmingham's Moor Street station.

These units are maintained at West Midlands Trains' Birmingham depot at Tyseley. On 11 October 2014, No. 172219 has just left the local station there and passes its home depot and heads for Birmingham.

Class 172/3

A few minutes later, sister unit No. 172337, a three-car set, is seen heading in the opposite direction and is about to pass through Tyseley station.

A total of fifteen three-car Class 172/3 units are also operating in the West Midlands. On 11 October 2014, one of these units, No. 172340, calls at Stourbridge Junction station.

On 15 February 2015, No. 172345 approaches journey's end as it terminates at Worcester Shrub Hill station. It is seen passing some of that station's surviving semaphore signals.

Class 175/0

A total fleet of twenty-seven Class 175 units were ordered by North West Trains. Built by Alstom in Birmingham, they are now in the hands of Arriva Trains Wales and are maintained at their depot in Chester. On 9 December 2015, No. 175003 has just come off the depot and is stabled opposite the station platforms, ready for its next working.

The Class 175/0 subclass contains a fleet of eleven two-car units. On Sunday 12 November 2017, several members of the class have stabled at Carmarthen overnight. This early morning view shows No. 175009 (on the left) and No. 175002 (on the right), both of which will soon be in service. A stabled Class 150, No. 150255, also stands in the centre, between the two Class 175s.

These units operate on most services across Wales from the south (as above) to the north, as in this photograph. No. 175006 arrives at Llandudno Junction on a late-running North Wales Coast service to Holyhead on 14 June 2018.

Class 175/1

A further sixteen three-car units, classified 175/1s, made up the Alstom order. On 10 July 2014, No. 175109 departs from Manchester's Piccadilly station on a service to Carmarthen.

Many of these services use the Marches Line along the border between Wales and England. On 15 July 2015, No. 175110 is platformed at Newport so that it can head north on its journey to Holyhead.

The Class 175s are also the regular performers on services along the North Wales Coast from Holyhead and Llandudno to Manchester. On 4 July 2013, No. 175116 has just terminated in one of the through platforms at the city's Piccadilly station.

Class 180

Similar to the Class 175s, these units were ordered at the turn of the century by First Great Western. Not without their problems, they were then handed back to their leasing company, Angel Trains, only to be given a second chance a few years later. They were introduced on Cotswold Line services in 2012. On 28 September 2016, No. 180103 passes Acton Main Line on one such service.

A year later, on 14 November 2017, stablemate No. 180104 passes South Moreton, near Didcot Parkway. Two coaches bear the 'Great Western legends' livery.

First Hull Trains also have a fleet of six of these Class 180 units operating on their services between London and Hull. On 27 January 2016, No. 180109 heads south through Newark North Gate on a King's Cross service.

The other operator currently employing these five-car Class 180 units is Grand Central. It has recently swapped its small fleet of High Speed Train power cars and coaching stock, and as a result it has increased its Class 180 pool to eight members. They work on services out of London King's Cross to both Sunderland and Bradford. On 16 February 2018, No. 180114 *Kirkgate Calling* arrives at Doncaster on a service to Bradford Interchange.

Class 185

First TransPennine Express (FTPE) ordered a total of fifty-one three-car units from Siemens in 2003. They had all entered service by January 2007. First-numbered No. 185101 is seen here at Darlington on 13 June 2013, working a northbound service to Newcastle.

FTPE provide a frequent service across the Pennines through Leeds station. On 23 June 2015, No. 185123 waits to leave the Yorkshire city to head westbound with a service to Liverpool's Lime Street station, via Manchester.

On the opposite side of the Pennines, No. 185126 is seen at Manchester Piccadilly on 14 November 2012. At the time all FTPE services to and from Manchester Airport reversed in the terminating platforms here.

In the last couple of years, FTPE has introduced a completely new corporate identity on its Class 185 fleet. Sporting its new colours, No. 185132 approaches Edale on 20 March 2018, shortly after a snowfall on the hills. It is on a Manchester Airport to Cleethorpes service.

FTPE Class 185 units have no through gangways. Despite this, they are sometimes seen in pairs, as this view of Barnetby on 5 July 2018 demonstrates. On this occasion, No. 185137 is seen leading No. 185147 as they head towards Cleethorpes on another working from Manchester Airport. The rear unit is not in passenger use.

Further north, the reopened station at Yarm, on Teesside, is served by FTPE Class 185 units with an hourly service to and from Middlesbrough. On 16 April 2018, No. 185150 calls on an eastbound working.

Class 220

The Class 220 and 221 'Voyager' units were the replacements for both ageing HSTs and the even older Class 47s and coaching stock. They were originally used by Virgin Trains from 2001 onwards. Since 2007, however, they have been a key part of the CrossCountry franchise and are found right across the UK, from Penzance to Aberdeen. On 9 May 2018, Class 220 unit No. 220004 passes Northam while heading towards Southampton Central.

Many of CrossCountry Trains' services to and from the West Country terminate at Bristol Temple Meads. One of their thirty-four four-car units, No. 220010, has just terminated on arrival on 22 February 2018.

At the opposite end of the country, No. 220031 stands at Glasgow Central on 9 April 2015. It will return south of the border via Edinburgh and the East Coast Main Line.

These units stable overnight at various points on the CrossCountry network, including at Eastleigh. On the morning of 16 July 2018, No. 220033 reverses in that station after leaving the depot there. It will run empty coaching stock to Bournemouth to commence its day's passenger diagram.

Class 221

This class of chiefly five-car diesel electric multiple units have been classified as 'Super Voyagers'. This is because, unlike their Class 220 counterparts, they were built with a tilting facility to enable higher speeds on curved tracks. One of these, No. 221107 *Sir Martin Frobisher,* operated by Virgin Trains, arrives at Crewe on 29 January 2015. It is on a London Euston to Chester service.

Heading in the opposite direction, Virgin Trains' No. 221118 approaches Rugeley Trent Valley on 18 July 2016 with a London Euston-bound service.

The CrossCountry Trains-operated sets have had this tilting mechanism disabled. On 31 May 2017, one of their units, No. 221126, arrives at Par while working the 09.27 to Glasgow Central.

Like their Class 220 counterparts, the Class 221s outstable at various points on the network, including Laira depot, in Plymouth. On 17 November 2017, No. 221127 passes through Newton Abbot on an empty stock working from Laira to Exeter. This unit will start its service day heading north from Exeter St Davids.

Pairs of Virgin Trains' examples are often found on Euston to Glasgow Central via the West Midlands services. On 28 June 2017, one such pairing sees No. 221142 *Bombardier Voyager* leading a northbound service through Stafford.

For many years, the two driving cars from unit No. 221144 were stored at Bombardier's Central Rivers depot near Barton-under-Needwood. They were returned to service as part of a four-car formation for CrossCountry Trains to give an extra train for service. This was achieved by reducing other five-car units to four cars. On 20 February 2018, the newly formed unit passes South Moreton, near Didcot Parkway, with a northbound service.

Class 222/0

Built originally for the Midland Main Line, the Class 222 'Meridians' were introduced from 2003 onwards. They are operated by East Midlands Trains (EMT) today, having seen some unit rearrangements in terms of the number of coaches in each. Six seven-car sets are now in use, including No. 222001 *The Entrepreneur Express,* which is seen here passing Oakley, north of Bedford, on 3 July 2018.

With a maximum speed of 125 mph, these seven-car units primarily work the hourly fast London St Pancras to Sheffield services, recently having displaced the operator's HSTs on these services. On 19 October 2015, No. 222004 *Children's Hospital Sheffield* stands at Sheffield, waiting to work a southbound service to St Pancras.

In its early days out on test, No. 222008 (now named *Derby Etches Park*) pauses at Market Harborough on 16 April 2004. At this time it was carrying a Midland Mainline livery.

The seventeen five-car units are usually found on services between St Pancras, Nottingham and Corby, as well as on the slower stopping services to Sheffield. On 20 May 2016, No. 222022 *Invest in Nottingham* waits to leave Corby on its return journey to St Pancras.

Class 222/1

The four four-car units that now supplement the EMT fleet were originally in use with Hull Trains. They are now maintained at EMT's Etches Park depot in Derby. No. 222101 stands at Derby station between duties on 16 May 2017.

On Fridays, one of these four-car unit steps up to replace the more usual Class 156 or 158 units covering some local 'Ivanhoe' services between Leicester, Nottingham and Lincoln. On 13 April 2018, No. 222102 pulls away from Loughborough on one such northbound working.

Class 230

The Class 230, or 'D' Train, was built by Viva Rail from converted former London Underground stock. An initial trial prior to their proposed use on the Coventry to Nuneaton service met with a premature end. Unit No. 230001 is seen here at Coventry on 4 January 2017, shortly after suffering fire damage. Despite this setback, Viva Rail have maintained faith in this conversion project. Three similar units are scheduled to take over Marston Vale services from Bletchley to Bedford at the end of 2018.

Class 950

Built in 1987, No. 950001 is the sole unit that was purpose-built for Network Rail, rather than a passenger train operator. It was built with the same bodyshell as a Class 150/1 passenger unit and is in regular use as a Track Assessment Unit. It is seen here heading south towards Bedford station while working from Derby to Bletchley on 4 March 2017.